Early Days with JESUS

God's wonderful world

The Ross family

Mum · Matthew · Dad · Gran Ross · Grandpa Ross · Nan Drew · Shags · Ben · Kate · Sparks

Published and produced by CWR, Waverley Abbey House, Waverley Lane, Farnham, Surrey GU9 8EP
Writer: Jenny King; Drawings: Harold King   Typeset by Watermark, Honing, Norfolk   Printed by Crusade Printing
ISBN 1—85345—000—6

NATIONAL DISTRIBUTORS
AUSTRALIA: Christian Marketing Pty Ltd., PO Box 154, N. Geelong, Victoria 3215. Tel: (052) 786100.
CANADA: Christian Marketing Canada Ltd., PO Box 7000, Niagara on the Lake, Ontario LOS 1TO. Tel: 416 641 0631.
EIRE: Scripture Union Book & Music Centre, 40 Talbot Street, Dublin 1. Tel: 363764.
MALAYSIA: Salvation Book Centre, (M) Sdn.Bhd, 23 Jalan SS2/64, 47300 Petaling Jaya, Selangor.
NEW ZEALAND: CWR (NZ), PO Box 4108, Mount Maunganui 3030. Tel: (075) 757412.
SINGAPORE: Alby Commercial Enterprises Pte Ltd., Garden Hotel, 14 Balmoral Road, Singapore 1025.
SOUTHERN AFRICA: CWR (Southern Africa), PO Box 43, Kenilworth 7745, RSA. Tel: (021) 7612560

How to use Early Days

Early Days has been designed to help parents to teach simple Bible truths in an exciting and practical way.

Choose a quiet area to work and have the materials (if any) needed for the activity at hand. You will find it most helpful to use the Good News Bible as this is the version that the *Early Days* notes are based upon.

Read the Bible verse and then the story, and try to involve your child as much as possible. Encourage him/her to talk about the reading and the story and add your own comments. Try to help your child understand the theme.

Take time to do the activity for the day, but don't worry if you can't finish it or if you miss a few days. It's better to "get together" every other day for a longer time than to rush every day.

After you have completed the activity, say the prayer at the bottom of the page. Encourage your child to add to this prayer time, perhaps including people or situations that you think are relevant.

Harold and Jenny King

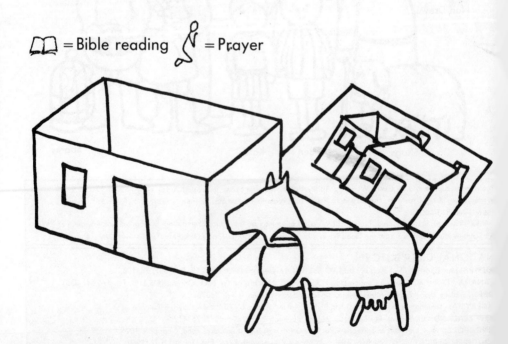 = Bible reading   = Prayer

In the beginning, God made the world.

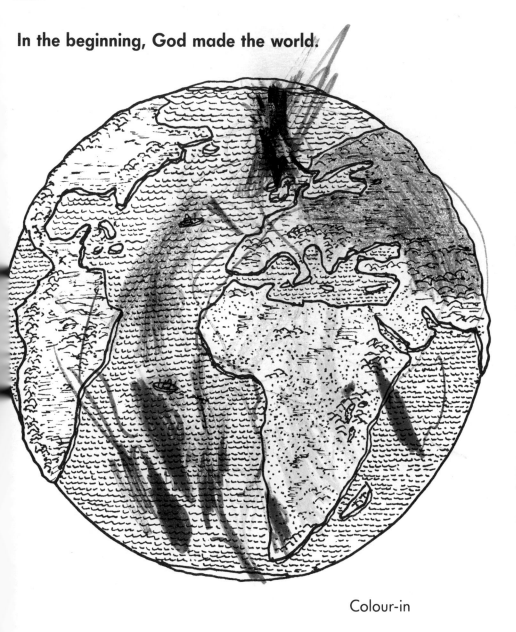

Colour-in

 Thank You, God, for making the world.

Then God made the sea.

Cut out patches of blue from old magazines to make a sea collage.

 Thank You, God, for the sea.

After making the world, God made the plants and trees to make it beautiful.

Find the right homes for these plants.

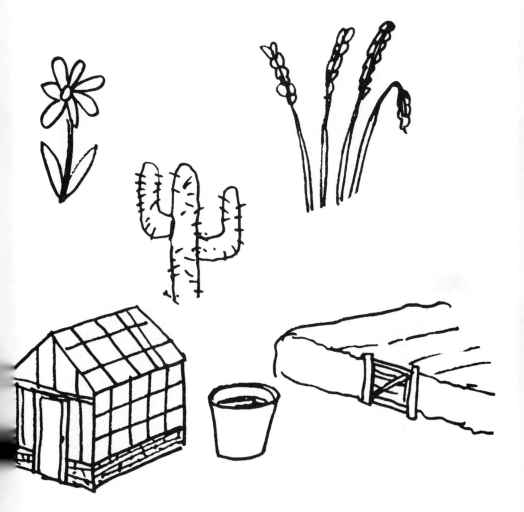

 Thank You, God, for making a beautiful world.

God then made the birds and fishes.

Colour all the fishes blue and all the birds red.

Thank You, God, for the birds and fishes.

📖 Genesis 1:24-25

After the birds and fishes, God made the animals to live on the land.

Draw lines to make pairs.

Thank You, God, for animals.

God made a man and woman to take care of the world.

Cut out man and woman (see last page) and stick to picture.

1

 Thank You, God, for making Adam and Eve.

A long time afterwards, God sent people to different parts of the world.

Help these people to get to their new homes.

Thank You, God, for all the different people in Your world.

This is the Ross family.

Colour-in

Thank You, God, for my family.

God sent Jesus to tell people about Him. This is Jesus' family.

Colour-in

 Dear Jesus, please take care of my family.

It's good to know we are all part of God's family.

me

Colour-in

 Thank You, Jesus, that I am part of Your family.

📖 Ecclesiastes 2:4-6

The Ross family live in a house. It has three bedrooms, a bathroom, lounge and kitchen-diner. They also have a garden to play in. What sort of house do you live in?

Colour-in

Thank You, God, for my house.

In Jesus' time, most houses only had one room. The animals lived at one end and the family lived at the other. There was a raised platform where they slept. When it was hot at night, they often slept on the roof.

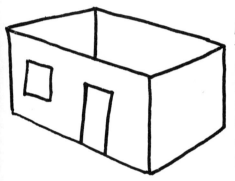

Make a model house

You will need a shoe box or similar. Cut out holes for windows and door. Inside, cut part of the lid to make the raised area where the family lived. Stick the inside of a match box for the manger from which the animals ate their food.

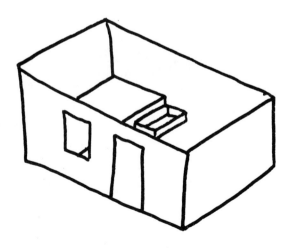

 Thank You, God, for all the different homes people make.

The Rosses have nice neighbours next door. Claire often pops in for a cup of tea and sometimes takes Ben and Kate to school and playschool.

In which houses do these neighbours live?

 Thank You, God, for neighbours.

John 15:12

Old Mrs Lloyd is very kind and Mum often gets her pension for her and does odd bits of shopping.

Can you name all the things on the list?

Dear Jesus, show me how I can be helpful.

Jesus tells us that everyone is our neighbour, not just the people next door, or across the road.

Colour-in

 Dear Jesus, help me to be a kind neighbour.

Looking out of the window, Ben and Kate can see the whole of the street they live in – not only the people but also the crossing, the traffic lights and the shop on the corner.

Make a street scene (see last page).   2

 Thank You, God, for my street and the people who live in it.

Ben and Kate live in a town, which is a place with lots of houses, shops and factories.

Cut out pictures of buildings from magazines.

 Dear Jesus, please keep me safe when there are lots of cars and people about.

When the weather is fine, Mum takes Ben and Kate to the park.

ck on wool for swing ropes.

Thank You, God, for nice days in the park.

When the weather is fine, Mum takes Ben and Kate to the park.

...k on wool for swing ropes.

Thank You, God, for nice days in the park.

 Proverbs 23:22

On the way home, they call at Nan's flat for a drink and a biscuit.

Draw a picture of your favourite snack.

 Please, God, keep old people safe.

Sometimes at weekends, Dad takes Ben and Kate swimming. Ben can just about swim on his own, but Kate still uses armbands. It's great fun, but Kate doesn't like it when people splash!

Cut out (see last page) and cut slot to 'swim'.   3

 Dear Jesus, help me to be kind and thoughtful.

Acts 2:42, 44

Nan goes to the same church as all the Ross family. They have lots of freinds there. It's good to feel part of God's family.

Draw a picture of your church.

Thank You, God, that I am part of Your family.

Gran and Grandpa live in the country with lots of fields and trees all around. Just down the road is the village which is only a few houses, a church, and a small shop.

Stick on scraps for leaves.

 Thank You, God, for the countryside You made.

Gran and Grandpa live on a farm. They keep ducks, chickens, cows and sheep.

Make a cow from a toilet roll and straws.

 Dear Jesus, please keep farmers safe as they look after the animals.

In their fields they grow wheat, some cabbages, and lots of grass for the animals.

Finger paint a picture of fields.

Thank You, God, that You provide food for everyone.

Matthew 2:19-21, 23. Luke 2:39

Jesus lived in a village called Nazareth, which is in the hills near Lake Galilee.

Colour-in

 Dear God, thank You for Jesus.

Matthew 2:19-23, 22; Luke 2:39a

Jesus lived in a village called Nazareth, which is in the hills near Lake Galilee

Colour in

Dear God, thank You for Jesus.

A stream runs through Gran and Grandpa's farm. The ducks enjoy swimming in it and Ben and Kate paddle and fish in it when they go to stay.

Help the children to catch the fish.

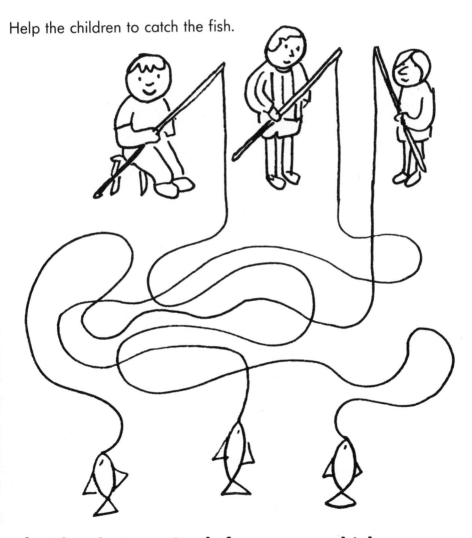

 Thank You, God, for water which we can enjoy.

The stream flows into a big river, which runs into the sea. Ben and Kate went to the seaside for their holidays.

Stick on silver paper for water.

Thank You, God, for holidays.

Psalm 104:24-26

Ben and Kate live in England, which is an island, so there is sea all around it.

What do you think an island looks like? Draw a picture.

 Thank You, God, for the sea and the fish that live in it.

 Psalm 98:4-9

England is only a small part of the world. There are many more countries with sandy deserts, high mountains and large lakes.

Colour-in

 Thank You, God, that You created so many different places.

📖 Psalm 95:1-7

Isn't it good that God made such a variety of places for His people to live in?

What places are these?

I _ _ _ _ _

M _ _ _ _ _ _ _ _ _

S _ _ _ _ _ _ _

C _ _ _ _ _ _ _ _ _ _

 Thank You, God, that You made me.

1

2

3

Literal Art & Signwriting

© Wayne Tanswell 2012

First published in Great Britain by
Tanswell Publications 2012
4 Kersey Avenue, Great Cornard, Sudbury, Suffolk CO10 0DZ

Printed by
The Lavenham Press Ltd
Arbons House, 47 Water Street, Lavenham, Suffolk CO10 9RN

ISBN No: 978-0-9562463-2-5

A lot of artists are offered advice on what to produce just to get accepted. What I create differentiates me from other artists and challenges the aesthetics of pictorial and landscape paintings. Therefore, I am not looking for advice on what to produce just to be accepted.

Since 1980 I have worked as a Traditional Sign Writer, my art also consists of painting letters. The images in this book are a combination of my art and signwriting.

Literal Art & Signwriting

Writing Wrongs,

Humorous & Thought Provoking

ihaveo

pinions

ofmyo

wnstro

ngopin

ionsBU

tidonta

lwaySa

greewit

Hthem

When I decided to write this book, I did not want to reconstruct my past just to fill out the pages; neither did I want to brush aside the true and sometimes colourful anecdotes which include my appalling grammar and spelling. However, I think it's important to address the fact that as my time in compulsory education drew to a close, I didn't really know what I wanted to do in terms of earning a living, but I knew I wanted to do something creative.

Casting my mind back to eighteen months prior to leaving school, I had a part time job working at a local bus company depot, sweeping out busses every evening. It was whilst working at this depot that I first met a traditional sign writer. Whenever he was working, I made a point of watching him paint. One day he asked me what I was going to do when I left school. I replied 'I would like to do your job.' He told me that if I wanted to be a sign writer, then I had better do well at school and pass my exams.

Don't say the World owes you
a living, the World was here
first. The World owes You
Nothing